GYMNASTICS
GIRLS ROCKING IT

GLEN F. STANLEY and ANN WESLEY

ROSEN
PUBLISHING

NEW YORK

Published in 2016 by The Rosen Publishing Group, Inc.
29 East 21st Street, New York, NY 10010

Copyright © 2016 by The Rosen Publishing Group, Inc.

First Edition

Library of Congress Cataloging-in-Publication Data
Stanley, Glen F.
Gymnastics : girls rocking it / Glen F. Stanley and Ann Wesley. – First Edition.
     pages cm. – (Title IX rocks! Play like a girl)
Includes index.
Audience: Grades: 7-12.
ISBN 978-1-5081-7037-2 (Library bound)
1. Gymnastics for girls–Juvenile literature. I. Wesley, Ann. II. Title.
GV464.S73 2016
796.4408352–dc23
                                                                    2015024380

Manufactured in China

CONTENTS

In 1972, Congress passed Title IX of the Education Amendments of 1972. It states, "No person in the United States shall, on the basis of sex, be excluded from participation in, be denied the benefits of, or be subject to discrimination under any education program or activities receiving Federal financial assistance." Since its passage, girls have been given more opportunities to participate in sports, including gymnastics. In recent years the explosion of female participation in sports has been so dramatic that the days of girls standing on the sidelines watching or performing just for pure entertainment value are long gone.

It's been more than forty-three years since Title IX, and there has been much progress in young women's participation in sports and gender equality in education, athletics, and the workplace. According to a *U.S. News* report in 2012, there was a 545 percent rise in female involvement in college sports since 1972 and a 979 percent rise in female participation in sports in high school. The influence of Title IX on education programs has been global. Some of these effects include an increase in the number of women who are pursuing careers aimed mostly at men, such as those in technology and science. Today, many girls and young women can train in jobs that were once offered only to boys or young men, such as woodworking or engineering, and vice versa. Because of Title IX, boys now can take

A high school girls' gymnastics team competes in the vault at a state championship event. Since the passage of Title IX in 1972, there has been a 979 percent increase in girls' participation in high school sports.

home economics or sewing classes without discrimination. In addition, Title IX made it illegal to ban pregnant students from school. Female teachers and professors are more common today than they were in 1972. Before Title IX, it was very challenging for girls and women to obtain athletic scholarships. Title IX has enabled more girls and women who are active in sports to have self-confidence in competing both athletically and academically. Many people credit

Title IX and federal funding of educational programs for the U.S. women's soccer team's win at the 2015 Women's World Cup.

A case could be made that participation in sports at the high school level helps a girl gain access to college and a career. The National Federation of State High School Associations stated in 2008 that young women who participated in athletics programs were more likely to graduate from high school, have very good grades, and perform at a higher level on standardized tests than nonathletes. A 2010 paper published by the National Bureau of Economic Research reported "being a high school athlete was associated with 14 percent higher wages for women." The Centers for Disease Control and Prevention's National Center for Health Statistics has stated that obesity, as a children's health epidemic, is particularly problematic in girls, especially girls of color. A 2006 National Center for Health Statistics report said, "Of girls aged 12 to 19, 23.8% of African-American girls and 14.6% of white girls are overweight." According to most medical researchers, routine physical activity can help to bring down the risk of obesity for teenagers.

The reason for taking up a sport such as gymnastics, however, should be much less complicated than these factors. You should perform gymnastics simply because you enjoy it.

The key to gymnastics, experts say, is doing something extremely difficult and making it look easy. There's certainly nothing easy about standing on a four-inch-wide (10-centimeter-wide) piece of wood four feet (1.2 meters) off the ground, flipping your body into the air to twist and turn, and then landing perfectly on that beam without a wobble. And there's nothing easy about running at full speed, jumping on a springboard, and vaulting high into the air to somersault twice and land without wavering. Yet when performed at the highest level, the sport looks graceful and effortless.

Women's gymnastics in its earliest form wasn't a sport. It

combined dance and acrobatics and dates back to the days of the pharaohs. Gymnastics as a sport dates back to ancient Greece where men alone competed in the earliest Olympic Games. Thousands of years later, in the late 1800s, women began using gymnastics as a means of physical fitness. In 1928, they participated in exhibitions at the Olympics.

Competition as it is known today didn't really catch on until the 1950s, when gymnasts' individual skills were first judged in the Olympics. The first female gymnastics star was Hungarian Agnes Keleti. In the 1952 Summer Olympic Games in Helsinki, Finland, she earned a gold medal in gymnastics floor exercise, a silver medal in team competition, and a bronze medal on the uneven bars. Four years later at the Summer Olympics in Melbourne, Australia, Keleti won another gold medal. In the same decade, Larisa Latynina and Vera Caslavska also made their marks on the world of gymnastics.

During the 1972 Summer Olympics, the sport underwent an amazing transformation when a Soviet teenager named Olga Korbut stunned a worldwide audience by letting go of the high uneven bar, executing a half-backward somersault, and catching the apparatus on her way down. In another event, spectators were left equally astonished when Korbut performed a back flip on the balance beam—a common event nowadays, but then the first ever to be performed in competition.

Four years after Korbut's remarkable performance, she was almost overshadowed by another astonishing teen, Romanian Nadia Comaneci. Comaneci displayed such an extraordinary degree of grace and athleticism that she earned seven perfect 10.0 scores in the 1976 Olympics in Montreal, Canada.

In the next four decades the sport of gymnastics moved from having a few women performing amazing feats to every serious gymnast working to make each routine more difficult, stunning, and dangerous. With each competition, whether it was Mary Lou Retton dominating; Kerri Strug, despite being injured in the 1996 Olympics in Atlanta, displaying triumphant courage in performing the vault; or Simone Biles prevailing as the individual all-around champion in the 2014 World Championships in Nanning, China, the bar of greatness is raised a bit higher and the skills become a lot harder to master. In 2008, in the Olympic Games in Beijing, China, and in 2012, in the Olympic Games in London, England, a new system and revised rules for scoring gymnastic routines were used. The new rules placed less importance on a gymnast's artistry than on her technical abilities. The new scoring rules have all but eliminated the high point of the sport's achievement, the perfect 10.0 score. Today a difficulty score and execution score with certain point values are combined to result in a total score. The difficulty score is the total value given for the ten most difficult skills, and credit is given for connections and element requirements, or those skills and elements that are necessary in a routine. An execution score is for the execution, artistry, composition, and technique of the routine. The execution score starts at 10.0 points, and deductions are made for errors and faults. A competitor's score can no longer be a maximum of 10.0 points; a very good score is now considered to be in the 15.0 to 16.0 points range.

This resource will examine some of the fundamentals of the sport and aspects that inspire those who dedicate their childhoods to improving their gymnastic skills.

CHAPTER ONE

GYMNASTICS BODY TYPES AND AGE

At a young age, many girls frequently have a natural interest in gymnastics. For these girls, that interest might simply consist of turning cartwheels in the yard on summer days, kicking up a handstand against a wall, taking early tumbling classes at a YMCA, or participating in cheerleading programs. A lot of them leave gymnastics behind as they enter womanhood.

For centuries, though, there have been women who never grew out of their love of gymnastics. Agnes Keleti was one of them. When she won that first gold medal in 1952, she was thirty-one years old, and when she won her second in 1956, she was thirty-five. Larissa Latynina and Vera Caslavska competed until they were thirty-two and twenty-six years old, respectively.

But these women are rarely mentioned among the sport's greatest athletes. Their accomplishments have been overshadowed in

Larisa Latynina of the Soviet Union competes in the individual all-around event at the Tokyo Olympics in 1964. She won the silver medal, nearly two months before her thirtieth birthday.

gymnastics history by the performances of tiny teenagers such as Olga Korbut, Nadia Comaneci, Mary Lou Retton, Shannon Miller, Shawn Johnson, Nastia Liukin, Daniela Silivas, Nellie Kim, Svetlana Khorkina, and many present-day athletes. Most of these young gymnasts retire in their early twenties or even sooner.

When these new stars showed the world that a four-foot-eleven-inch (1.5-m), eighty-five-pound (38.6-kilogram) girl could perform daring, graceful, incredibly athletic moves on gymnastics apparatus and in floor exercise, the sport was changed, perhaps forever. Judges and coaches came to believe that to compete at the highest level and to maneuver their bodies in the way that these girls had, athletes had to be small. And the younger they were, the smaller their bodies usually were.

In 1956, when Keleti competed, the average U.S. gymnast was nineteen years old, stood five feet four inches (1.6 m) tall, and weighed 124 pounds (56 kg). By the early 1990s, the average age had dropped to sixteen, the height to four feet nine inches (1.45 m), and the weight to just over 80 pounds (36.3 kg). Girls as young as twelve or thirteen were competing. The International Gymnastics Federation realized that such fierce competition wasn't healthy or safe for girls who were still growing. In 1996, the federation stated that a girl had to be fifteen years old to participate in world competition. In 1997, the minimum age for women's gymnastics at a world championship or the Olympic Games was raised to sixteen.

Fourteen-year-old Nadia Comaneci swings on the uneven bars, on which she earned the perfect score of 10.0 and the gold medal, at the Montreal Olympics in 1976.

More important than age in gymnastics are body shape and size. Female bodies are mainly divided into three types: heavy, thin and muscular, or slim. Most girls do not fit one type exclusively. But the unique body type a girl has may determine which events in gymnastics she will have a better chance at mastering. For example, those girls with a combination body leaning toward a heavier shape and size often are more successful in balance beam because of a lower center of gravity. Girls with thin, muscular shapes often excel on the vault or uneven bars, which involve flipping and twisting the body over quickly.

THE BODY TYPES OF SOME CHAMPION GYMNASTS

In 2012, at a height of four feet eleven inches (1.5 m) and a weight of 90 pounds (41 kg), American Gabby Douglas won the gold medal for the individual all-around gymnastics event at the London Summer Olympics. As Andrew Mooney, a journalist for the website Boston.com, reported in his study on the bodies of some of the champion gymnasts,

U.S. gymnast Simone Biles, age seventeen, performs on the balance beam while at the World Championships in Nanning, China.

unusual body types are often found in gymnastics today. But that was not the case until about 1980, when Maxi Gnauck (an East German who tied Nadia Comaneci for the silver medal in the women's individual all-around at the Moscow Summer Olympics in 1980) was the first competitor under five feet (1.5 m) to medal in the women's individual all-around competition. In Mooney's study, he found that heights of champion gymnasts have been fairly constant over the past sixty years and that 78 percent are "within three inches of five feet tall." His data point to a downward trend from an average of approximately 120 pounds (54.4 kg) in the 1950s and 1960s to fewer than 100 pounds (45.4 kg) in today's sport. Based on his research, Mooney concluded that "the average medal-winning gymnast in the all-around is 19.6 years old, measures 5'1" and weighs 103 pounds."

The fact that many of the gymnasts in international competition are tiny doesn't mean that only small girls can enjoy the sport. Just as a four-foot-eleven-inch (1.5-m), 85-pound (38.6-kilogram) girl would need spectacular skills to play professional basketball, a six-foot-two-inch (2-m), 176-pound (80-kg) girl is not likely to be a top-ranked gymnast. But any girl who works hard can accomplish other goals in gymnastics. Walk into any gymnastics school or sporting event and you'll see girls from preschool to college age—and older women as well—performing gymnastic skills in competition, for fun and as part of cheerleading, dance, and other sports. From 2006 to 2013, about five million people in the United States participated in gymnastics, according to Statista.com. In 2014, the National Collegiate Athletic Association (NCAA) listed fewer than one hundred schools at the college level offering gymnastics programs in Divisions I, II, and III. Only a handful of gymnasts make it to the international level. For the rest, the sport provides exercise, enjoyment, and competitiveness.

"I think it's possible to be five feet nine inches [1.8 m] and be a good gymnast," said one fourteen-year-old competitor, standing just five feet one inch (1.6 m). "That's just my personal opinion. It

Russian gymnast Svetlana Khorkina performs on the uneven bars. In the sport, Khorkina is considered to be tall in height at five feet five inches (1.65 m).

might affect you slightly, but you can overcome it. Tall gymnasts look more impressive doing the same skills. It just means you might have to work harder." A gymnast's mother adds, "Being small makes it easier to make fast rotations because your body mass tends to be in tighter to center."

Many coaches believe the best age to start a girl in gymnastics training is between two and four years old. At that age, children are generally interested in tumbling and are still developing their sense of self. They usually don't have the fears of falling or getting hurt that older students can have. Beyond that starting level, girls enter classes, not by age, but by skill level. Beginner classes teach the basics and let the students begin more extensive work on the balance beam, uneven bars, vault, and different floor exercises. When a girl is ready, she moves to the intermediate or advanced levels where a set of skills is put together into a continuous routine.

If a girl decides to move into competition, she will be evaluated and placed in a skill division from 1 to 10. Competition levels range from 5 to 10, with those reaching the top moving on to the elite or

Two young girls in a beginner's class practice a movement on the balance beam. The typical age to begin gymnastics is from two to four years old.

Olympic level. Many communities support strong level 2 to 4 programs through Amateur Athletic Union (AAU) organizations.

When a girl moves into the upper levels of competition, she usually needs to make a serious commitment to gymnastics, sacrificing some of her social activities to focus on practice several times each week. Sometimes a gymnast spends as much time practicing as she does in school! She learns lessons in anatomy, balance, sports medicine, and the laws of gravity. Gymnasts train their bodies to stretch and hold positions for several minutes. They learn to combine dance with athletics and maneuver their bodies around equipment, and they practice each move until it's perfect. Although athletes in other sports can still win after making mistakes—dropping a fly ball in softball or missing a jump shot in basketball—one tiny mistake in gymnastics will not only knock the athlete out of competition, it can result in serious injury. In 1998, a Chinese gymnast, Sang Lan, was left paralyzed after she fell during a practice session for a vault event for that year's Goodwill Games.

One twelve-year-old gymnast spends about eight hours every week in the gym. She's been with the sport for only a year. She knows she'll never make it to the Olympic Games but still enjoys her sport. "I really started too late to be an elite. I'm practically the only one who is twelve and still on level 4. I don't care, though. It doesn't matter how old you are, how tall or short you are, how good you are. If you are having fun, then that's what counts." She also likes to set goals for herself and accomplish them. She also realizes that she is learning valuable life skills.

CHAPTER TWO

BUILDING STRENGTH, FLEXIBILITY, AND BASIC SKILLS

Common daily activities may be enough to build up a person's strength. In other cases, a coach may include sit-ups, push-ups, chin-ups, handstands, and other exercises in the individual's training. In certain cases, weight lifting also may be incorporated. No exercise program should be started without the advice and assistance of a trained professional. Doing these activities the incorrect way can result in muscle strain or serious injury.

Some basic strength exercises include:

- Simple push-ups (sometimes called girl-style push-ups): Lie on your stomach, legs together and arms bent so that your hands rest, palms down, on the floor next to your shoulders. Bend your knees and point your feet up. Push your body up until your arms are straight. Your back should stay straight and knees must stay on the floor. Lower your body back to the floor and repeat.

Doing girl-style push-ups regularly can help to strengthen the upper body and core muscles.

- Push-ups: Similar to simple push-ups but do not bend the knees. Put your toes on the floor and push your entire body up, keeping your back and legs straight. Some doctors don't think this move is safe for girls.
- Leg squat: Stand on one leg with your arms pointing out and your other leg held straight out, parallel with your arms at about hip level. Squat down on one leg and slowly stand back up, keeping your nonsupport leg held straight out. You can hold on to a chair to help keep your balance. Switch legs and repeat.
- Press: Stand with legs spread shoulder-width apart. Bend over straight and put your hands flat on the floor about eight to ten inches (20 to 25 cm) in front of you. Shift your weight onto your hands by raising up onto your toes and shifting your hips over

your shoulders. This will build strength and help you develop a solid handstand.

- Frog stand: Position yourself into a squat and place your hands, about shoulder width, on the floor in front of your feet, next to the toes. Move your knees so that they rest on the outside of your bent elbows, which will help support some of your body weight. Lean or tip forward until you can move your weight onto your hands so that your feet are raised off the floor. Gradually try to work up to holding the frog stand for one minute. This exercise helps to develop balance and muscle strength.

STRETCHING AND FLEXIBILITY

The more flexible her muscles become, the better range of motion a gymnast will have. However, there's a danger of muscles becoming too loose and, as a result, more open to injury. The younger a gymnast is, the easier it is for her to become flexible, but proper exercises and stretching can enable almost anyone to become more limber. The important thing to remember in any flexibility exercise is to move in a controlled manner rather than a fast, jerky way and to ease into the stretch rather than push through a point of pain.

Some basic flexibility exercises and stretches include:

- The split: Start by standing with one leg in front, bent at the knee, while the back leg stays straight. Lean forward until you can put your hands on the floor on each side of the front foot. Slowly push backward with your back leg until your front leg is straight. Slowly take some of the weight off your hands. With practice you will be able to get all the way down. Reverse position and split with the back leg in front this time. As you become more comfortable with this position, you will learn a right split (facing right), left split (facing left), and middle split (facing forward).

A young gymnast does a right split. Practicing a split helps develop flexibility and stretches the hamstrings, the muscles located at the back of the thigh.

- Back arch: Lie on your back, with your knees bent and your feet together tucked as close to your bottom as possible. Put your palms flat on the floor next to your shoulders with your thumbs pointing at your ears and your fingers pointing down toward your body. Using your arms, push up until your arms are straight. Then push up with your legs so that your whole body is arching like a bridge while your hands and feet stay on the floor.
- Hamstring stretch: You'll need a partner for this one. The girls sit facing each other as they press the bottoms of their feet together with legs together and stretched full out. Reach forward and hold hands, holding this position for several seconds. Hold the right hands, then left, then both.

When proper strength and flexibility movements have been learned, it's time to learn some basic skills.

FUNDAMENTAL SKILLS

There are some basic skills and moves that all beginner gymnasts need to be able to learn and become proficient in.

Forward Roll

This basic somersault must be mastered before you can go any further in gymnastics. Squat and rest your chin on your chest. Tuck your body into a ball, lift your rear end, and roll forward. End the move in the same squat position you started with. Be careful not to roll with such force that you drive your head into the mat. Keep your knees pulled in against your chest and close to your head.

Backward Roll

Squat in a ball with your arms against your sides and bent so the palms of your hands are next to your shoulders and facing up. Rock backward, staying tucked in a ball, and push against the mat with your hands to push over. End back in the squat position. You must roll fast and hard.

Cartwheel

Stand in an X-shape, arms and legs apart. Imagine a clock with your arms at 10:00 and 2:00 above your head. Your feet should be at 8:00 and 4:00. Keep your eyes set on the mat on the position you will hit and move in a straight line. If you start with your left foot out, then put your left hand out. If you start with the right foot, put the right hand out. Step forward and lunge with the leg, bend at the waist, and reach toward the mat with your hands while driving your back leg over your head. Land with your kick leg first, push with your hands, bring the other foot down, and stand. Your movement should be hand, hand, foot, and foot. The cartwheel can help in the process for the elements of round-offs and walkovers. It can also help in establishing balance and vertical alignment skills.

Handstand

This is a skill needed for most events and one of the first moves that must be mastered. It is important not only to be able to get into a straight handstand position but also to be able to hold that position for a minute or more. You see versions of the handstand in floor exercise, balance beam, and gymnastic routines.

Although it may seem the handstand is all about arm strength, leg muscles also are needed to kick the body up into position. The stomach and back keep the body in the proper position. One of the first things to learn is how hard to kick to get your body upright without having too much momentum and going all the way over.

Many gymnasts recommend doing handstands against a wall with your back and feet against the wall. Once in the handstand

When doing a handstand, make sure you have a padded surface under you. Both hands should be spaced apart about shoulder width and your fingers spread out a little and facing forward.

position, hold steady for as long as you can—starting with several seconds and gradually building up to a minute. As you get better and stronger, you can move away from the wall and rely on your strength alone to hold you up. Whenever you begin doing handstands away from the wall, it is important to have a spotter with you to make sure you don't fall and get hurt. A spotter should be strong enough to catch you and know enough about your sport to offer constructive advice.

To prevent bad habits from forming, some common mistakes should be avoided while learning handstands.

- Never place your hands wider or narrower than the width of your shoulders.
- Never arch your head back or forward.
- Always keep your stomach and middle of your body straight.
- Always keep your legs together and straight.

GYMNASTICS EQUIPMENT

Women's gymnastics revolves around four basic events: balance beam, floor exercise, uneven bars, and vault. With the exception of floor exercise, each event involves a piece of equipment or apparatus. The floor exercise is performed on mats, and the skills used there are carried into the other events. What follows is a description of each event and the skills needed to perform within it. Each gymnast will naturally have her favorite, but to be an all-around gymnast, action in each event is needed.

Floor Exercise

This is performed on a special mat measuring 40 feet (12 m) long and 40 feet (12 m) wide. Under the mat is a spring-enhanced floor.

Gymnasts perform their floor exercise to music and use the entire mat area to showcase tumbling and dance skills. Gymnasts must not step outside the boundaries of the mat and generally must complete a specific set of skills within ninety seconds. This doesn't give a girl much chance to think about her moves. Typical skills used in the floor exercise are tumbling interspersed with leaps, jumps, twists, turns, and dance moves. As with other routines, the action must be continuous and smooth. The gymnast must have excellent body control and make her skills look effortless.

Balance Beam

This is a 16-foot (5-m) long piece of wood that is 4 inches (10 cm) wide, set in a stand 4 feet (1 m) high. When gymnasts perform on the beam in competition, they must use the full length of the beam and must perform for one minute to a minute and a half. The routines must cover specific skills such as moving from a standing position to a kneeling or sitting position and getting back up smoothly. The most important elements of this event, other than staying on the beam, are demonstrating power and control while performing a smooth, diverse routine that includes

A coach helps a gymnast while practicing on the balance beam to keep her hips and shoulders square to the beam.

peaks or high points of skill. These peaks generally consist of put-ting two or more moves together in quick succession, such as a cartwheel, a back handspring, and a back flip.

The secret of a good beam performance is to keep your cen-ter of gravity over the beam at all times. This means the hips and shoulders must be square to the beam. Your feet should be turned out slightly and your toes can grip the side of the beam to help bal-ance. You should not be watching your feet—instead, you should keep your head up.

Uneven Bars

The uneven parallel bars are two bars of different heights sus-pended in a metal frame. They can be adjusted for each girl, but the low bar must be 148 centimeters (nearly 5 feet) tall, plus or minus 3 centimeters (1 in), while the high bar must be 228 centimeters (7.5 ft) tall, plus or minus 3 centimeters). (Some bars can be adjusted to a maximum of 150 centimeters [almost 5 ft] apart from each other.)

The object of the event is to swing around the bars and move from one to the other in a smooth, strong rhythm without stopping. A gymnast must have the courage and strength to let go of the bar, perform a skill, and catch the bar again. She must change hand-grips many times and must incorporate big moves with graceful swings. The gymnast must stay in complete control of her body so that she can stop the action, hold a move, and reverse direction. At the end of the routine, she must perform a tumbling dismount and land on steady feet.

Gymnasts use chalk (magnesium carbonate) on their hands to reduce the friction between the palms and the surface of the bars. Those who work out a great deal on bars may use leather handgrips on their palms to reduce friction and provide a more stable grip.

TAKING CARE OF RIPS

"Letting it rip," or to go at something full speed, is a good thing in most sports because you are giving it your all. However, in gymnastics, a rip is not a good thing. A rip is a tear in or removal of the skin caused by blisters that break open. Sometimes a small pocket in the skin can form and it fills with blood. Rips occur most commonly in uneven bar work because of the friction against the hands and some-times the wrists. Girls will generally develop calluses and some will use anything from moisturizing lotion to leather grips to try to keep their hands pro-tected. Rips, though, are a typical occurrence in this sport. Many times, they can be a result of a grip that is too tight. Elite gymnasts can get rips because they have callouses that are too big on their hands. (You can use a pumice stone to gently rub and remove the dead skin of the callous.)

When a rip occurs it must be treated properly to prevent infection. The open blister should first be washed with a gentle soap and warm water and dried. Soap may burn, but it is needed to clean the wound. The ripped area should then be bandaged and taped. If you don't have to continue practice, don't. If a rip happens during a meet or you need to continue practicing, make sure the area is taped properly so the tape doesn't roll up and cause more problems. After practice apply an antibiotic ointment and keep the area clean and covered until it heals. If there are any signs of infection, see a doctor immediately. Once new skin has formed over the rip, remember to use moisturizer on your skin to keep it from cracking or drying out.

Vault

Vaulting consists of a strong, fast run down a runway that measures 1 meter (3 ft) wide and no more than 25 meters (82 ft) long, with a springboard (also known as a beat board) and a padded "horse" (sometimes called a table) at the end.

The vaulting horse stands 120 centimeters (4 ft) tall and is 35 centimeters (1 ft) wide by 160 centimeters (5 ft) long.

The gymnast runs down the runway, then jumps on the springboard to give her enough power to make contact with the horse with her hands, timing it so that she can hit an exact spot, while her feet fly over the head. Pushing off the horse, she manages flips, twists, somersaults, and other acrobatic moves before landing on steady feet.

Vaults are grouped into four categories:
1. Forward approach vaults in which the body flips over to land facing forward. Flips are optional.
2. Forward approach vaults with a flip in landing flight. This move involves a backward or forward flip to land.
3. Vaults with a half turn onto the horse and a flip in landing flight.
4. Vaults (with or without flips) from a round-off onto the springboard.

A common fault in vaulting is having the arms positioned above the head while the feet are still on the springboard. The arms should come from behind and lift up and forward during the jump and takeoff (except

In the preflight phase of the vault, a gymnast keeps her legs together and straight and toes pointed, just before her hands touch the vault horse (which is also called the table).

with round-off entry vaults). Girls should practice this position on the floor before moving to the vault.

COMPETITION SCORING

Gymnastics competitions are judged and scored both as individual and team events. Each girl is required to perform a required number of specific moves on each piece of equipment. The Junior Olympic Code of Points and Women's Program Rules and Policies of the USA Gymnastics are usually used in state and national competitions. A gymnast usually starts with a 10.0 and has errors deducted from that value in tenths of points. Judging is subjective; that is, each judge has his or her own opinion of how well the skill was performed. There are guidelines for judges to use to try to make sure the scoring is fair, and judges must be very knowledgeable about the sport but, unlike many other sports, the score is based primarily on the opinion of the judges. Usually there are four judges, and the highest and lowest scores are dropped to provide a more objective total score. In USA Gymnastics competitions, there are four branches of competition: compulsory, optional, elite, and Xcel. In the first kind of Junior Olympic competition, there are compulsory competitions, which are levels 3–5. The second kind of Junior Olympic completion is called the optional, which includes levels 6–10. Elite gymnastics involves the best gymnasts in the sport, and these girls complete at the Olympic Games. Xcel competitions were developed by USA Gymnastics to offer individual flexibility to both gymnasts and coaches. This program provides girls of "varying abilities and commitment levels the opportunity for a rewarding gymnastics experience," according to the USA Gymnastics 2014–2015 Women's Program Rules and Policies. There are two types of routines in gymnastics—compulsory and optional.

Compulsory Program

In the compulsory routines, each gymnast must perform a required set of skills. Each skill must be executed in a specific order with the correct height, timing, and body position. All the gymnasts at the same level perform the same routine. Judges start scoring at a value of 10.0 and make deductions for each type of error detected, such as how the hand or foot is placed, the execution of a particular skill, or a fall.

Optional Level

In the optional routines, there are basic skills to be performed but they can be executed in different styles that make them more or less difficult. The difficulty ratings are regularly changed by the International Gymnastics Federation, the governing organization for the sport globally, as the sport evolves and athletes continue to add harder and harder skills to their routines. Every level has special requirements for the uneven bars, balance beam, and floor events, and each is worth a value of 0.5. There also are certain skills that are required in the gymnast's routine. Each of these skills is given a letter value for level of difficulty, with the "A" being the easiest skill. The start value is 10.0 and is given if the routine is performed perfectly. In some levels, such as level 9, a gymnast's starting value is 9.7 and she must earn an extra 0.3 by linking various skills together. As with compulsories, points are also subtracted for errors. The degree of difficulty a routine carries is determined prior to the event so that each judge does not individually decide how difficult the routine is. Optional levels 6–9 and Xcel gymnastics have restrictions on the difficulty of elements.

CHAPTER THREE

GYMNASTICS SAFETY AND RULES

As with participation in most sports, the safety of athletes is of the greatest concern at all times. Besides learning moves and use of equipment, there are several other subjects that gymnasts need to be aware of and learn about before committing to gymnastics. Make sure you know the benefits of good eating habits and the drawbacks about nutritional supplements. In addition, if your school or gymnastics club does not have information about how heat stress and dehydration can affect you while practicing or performing, make certain that you ask your coach or trainer about these factors. Your school should also have guidelines for the avoidance of head trauma and concussion injuries and have access to quick medical treatment, if necessary.

Before any gymnast first gets on the balance beam, grabs the uneven bars, or touches the horse, she must be able to perform the routine. Trying to learn the moves on a specific piece of apparatus will most often lead to serious injury. Many hours must be spent learning moves and mastering skills in a protected environment with a trained, experienced teacher or coach before trying them on your own.

Although parents may want to help a girl learn gymnastics and may volunteer to "spot" a daughter, that decision is unwise if the parent is not trained. A proper spotter knows how to guide the athlete through a move and is strong enough to support the gymnast. In the early stages of learning, the spotter may actually carry the girl through the motion while telling her how and where to place her hands, arms, legs, and feet.

Some gymnastics schools use a belt with ropes attached through pulleys as a spotting device. The coach can use the ropes

A trainer works with a gymnast who is using the uneven bars. Having a properly trained spotter on the bars while performing a new routine is essential for safety.

to lift the gymnast and help her maneuver through the routine. (Most schools require high school gymnasts to wear a safety collar during round-off entry vaults both in training and competition.) Other schools may use a landing pit, which is basically a large rectangular hole cut in the floor and filled with soft landing mats. It helps beginning gymnasts to know that they will land on a safer surface.

When it comes to actually learning the gymnastics moves, a girl must realize that this sport cannot be learned after only five minutes of instruction. To become a good gymnast, an athlete must put in several hours of work each week in addition to undergoing strength and flexibility training. Although younger girls often have less fear of tumbling or trying new skills, they often lack the attention span and discipline needed to participate in gymnastics.

Before attempting any routine, a girl and her coach should make sure she is strong enough. Before performing it on a piece of equipment, such as the balance beam, the gymnast should be able to perform the trick perfectly on a straight line on the floor. She should honestly decide whether she is nervous about doing the skill. If the answer is yes, she is likely not ready to try it on a piece of equipment yet. She should also take the time to mentally prepare for the skill. Many coaches say a skill must be performed eighty to a hundred times before it is "programmed" into the brain and the gymnast's body is trained to do the move.

Visualization is one of the primary elements of preparation in gymnastics. To understand the skill, a girl must be able to see herself doing it and then be able to describe it clearly. If she can't describe in her own words what she will do, she may not have a clear understanding of that specific skill. Before attempting the move, the girl should be able to tell the coach what position her arms and legs and body should be in during any part of the skill. Imagining doing the skill helps to develop focus and concentration.

Good preparation in a gymnastics routine includes visualizing the routine and being able to describe clearly the movements and positions in the routine.

It's important not to try to take on too much at one time. Learn a skill, master it, and then add new things. If you try to learn too many skills at one time, you'll have a basic knowledge of many but not be able to perform any well. Each gymnast moves at her own pace. You should feel pressure to improve your performance, but you shouldn't feel fear. If you are afraid to try something, it's often a signal that you don't understand the move or haven't mastered the skills you need.

So how do you know when you are ready to move on? One rule of thumb is to count how many times you do a move correctly in a practice session. You should perform the skill correctly on more than half of the attempts you make before you decide to add harder elements to it.

In gymnastics, as in any other sport, injuries are going to occur. A gymnast can take steps to reduce the chance of injury—using a spotter, understanding a move, stretching, staying focused—but sometimes the nature of the sport is going to lead to injuries. According to the Center for Injury Research and Policy in Columbus, Ohio, of the three million young people between the ages of six and seventeen who participate in gymnastics, more than 25,000

SIGNS AND SYMPTOMS OF CONCUSSION

When most people think of concussion, they think of players in football or hockey, where athlete collisions occur frequently. Although a concussion is not the most common injury in the sport of gymnastics, it is one of the most threatening. From data reported by the National Federation of State High School Associations' Injury Surveillance System, it is estimated that more than 140,000 high school athletes throughout the United States suffer a concussion annually. A concussion is also called a mild traumatic brain injury. It is usually brought on by a bump or blow to the head, but it can also be caused by any blow to your body that makes your head violently snap around and your brain hit the inside of your skull. The injury can result in damage to brain cells and lead to chemical changes in the brain. The signs and symptoms can last for just a few days or several months and longer. The Centers for Disease Control and Prevention (for an explanation of concussion and its danger signs and symptoms, see http://www.cdc.gov/headsup/basics/concussion_whatis.html) lists the following signs for a concussion that are noticed about the athlete by others:

- The athlete seems to be dazed or stunned.
- She is confused about what she is doing.

continued on page 36

continued from page 35

- She forgets the play or movement.
- She is unsure of the game/routine, score, or opponent.
- She moves in a clumsy way.
- She answers questions slowly.
- She loses consciousness.
- She shows a change in her behavior or personality.
- She cannot recall events that happened before the hit or injury.
- She cannot remember the events after the injury.

Symptoms of a concussion that are reported by the athlete include the following:
- A headache
- Nausea or vomiting
- Balance issues or dizziness
- Double vision or fuzziness
- Being sensitive to light or noise
- Feeling sluggish
- Feeling mentally groggy or foggy
- Memory problems or difficulty concentrating
- Confusion

Any coach or trainer who has a gymnast who is displaying any of these signs or symptoms should take that gymnast out of competition or practice and get her medical help immediately. As the popular saying goes: When in doubt, sit them out.

of them are treated for gymnastics-related injuries in U.S. hospital emergency rooms every year.

A young athlete needs to understand whether a pain is the result of normal activity or the result of an injury. When a gymnast first becomes involved in the sport, some degree of pain will almost certainly occur as muscles are stretched and used in a new way. That pain, though, is different from the more severe pain caused by an injury. When an injury occurs, gymnastics activity should stop until the injury can be assessed and a professional can advise whether it is safe to continue.

SOME COMMON INJURIES FOR GYMNASTS

Sprains are among the most common injuries in gymnastics. A sprain is a pulling or a tearing of a ligament connecting the bones at a joint.

Netteb Chantysha injured her knee on the vault at the World Championships in 2013. Her rehabilitation program included the uneven bars, the only apparatus she could then work on.

The intensity of the sprain can range from mild to severe. The more severe the sprain, the less likely it is the ankle will hold weight. The ligament may become partially or completely torn in severe sprains and will need to be treated by a doctor. Minor sprains can be treated with ice, to reduce swelling, and rest. The most common areas of sprain for gymnasts are those involving the ankles, wrists, knees, and backs.

Muscle strain is another common ailment for gymnasts. A muscle strain may occur when you overstretch or tear a muscle or tendon. Strains can usually be treated by resting and applying ice to the sore area. More severe strains may require a visit to the doctor.

Muscle soreness is inevitable in gymnastics and most other sports. Many times the pain doesn't set in until a couple of days after a hard workout. This is known as delayed onset muscle soreness. In normal exercise, tiny muscle fibers can tear when pulled, causing pain. These fibers will, however, rebuild in a day or two. This type of injury can usually be prevented by stretching well before and after exercise and by gradually working into a hard routine instead of going all out two minutes after entering the gym.

A more serious injury that can affect gymnasts is a stress fracture. This injury typically occurs because of continuing overuse of a joint. The main symptom of a stress fracture is pain. The most frequent places a stress fracture occurs are the leg bones and feet. Depending on the severity of the injury, treatments include rest, wearing a cast, and physical therapy.

Following these safety guidelines can help you prevent injury and enjoy your sport.

- Always stretch before starting a workout. Hold each stretch for at least thirty seconds. Always use an experienced spotter. A coach should spot gymnasts during all practice sessions when complex or challenging routines are being performed.
- Check the equipment to make sure it is properly maintained.

A gymnast stretches with a coach before a competition. Gymnasts should do stretching exercises before every practice workout and competition event to help prevent injuries.

- Make sure proper mats are being used and that they are placed correctly to pad landings.
- Avoid loose-fitting clothing that can get caught on equipment.
- Stay focused. An interruption in concentration or unnecessary distraction can cause a fall and lead to injury.

GYMNASTS, BODY IMAGE, AND EATING DISORDERS

In any discussion of gymnastics and safety, the issue of nutrition and eating disorders is always a concern. According to a 1992 American College of Sports Medicine study, eating disorders affected 62 percent of females in sports with an emphasis on being

U.S. gymnast Alexandra Raisman performs on the beam at the 2012 Olympic Games. Raisman is not insecure about her musclular body because it has made her the athlete she is today.

thin, including gymnastics. In gymnastics, points are awarded for the routine—but unfortunately, the athlete's appearance and body type still can influence judges.

The two main eating disorders affecting gymnasts are anorexia nervosa and bulimia nervosa. An anorexic condition consists of significant weight loss from excessive dieting. Anorexics often consider themselves overweight and try to avoid eating, even when their actual weight is well below medical standards. Like anorexia, bulimia is characterized by the desire to be thinner, even when a girl may already be underweight. But rather than an avoidance of food, bulimia involves binge eating—frantic overeating—following by forced vomiting or the overuse of laxatives. Those affected by either disease often suffer from low self-esteem, have a strong desire to be the best, and desperately want to please others. Athletes who have eating disorders can be at risk for having other medical issues, such as chemical imbalances and heart arrhythmias. Because they already are involved in demanding physical activities, they put a lot of pressure on their body organs. With an eating disorder, they can have an increased risk of sudden death because of cardiac arrest. Trainers and coaches, too, have to be more in tune with the dangers of eating disorders in the athletes they are working with.

For active athletes, not eating enough does not provide the body with enough energy to get through a routine or practice. Girls become light-headed and unbalanced and can faint. Long-term effects of eating disorders include organ failure and cardiac arrest. Gymnast Cathy Rigby, an Olympian in 1972, battled eating disorders for twelve years. Twice she faced death when she went into cardiac arrest. In the 1980s, elite gymnast Christy Henrich was told by a judge that she was too heavy to be the best. In attempts to control her weight, she developed anorexia and bulimia. She died in 1994 after her weight dropped to only 47 pounds (21 kg) and her organs failed. She was just twenty-two years old.

Warning signs of anorexia nervosa can include noticeable weight loss, excessive exercise, fatigue, depression, cold hands and feet, muscle weakness, obsession with food, regular excuses for not eating, unusual eating habits, discomfort around food, complaints about being fat, cooking for others but not eating, mood swings, irritability, evidence of vomiting, use of diet pills, irregular menstruation, fainting and dizziness, being secretive about eating habits, pale or pasty complexion, headaches, and low self-esteem.

Warning signs of bulimia can include binge eating, secretive eating, bathroom visits after eating, vomiting, use of laxatives and/or diet pills, weight fluctuations, swollen glands, broken blood vessels, excessive exercise, fasting, mood swings, depression, low self-esteem, self-worth determined by weight, negative thoughts about self after eating, fatigue, muscle weakness, tooth decay, irregular heartbeat, avoidance of restaurants or social events that involve food, and substance abuse.

Bulimia can cause a condition in some athletes called female athlete triad. The word "triad" refers to the three health problems that combine to appear in some girls and women, particularly in those who are in competitive sports. The three problems are disordered eating, loss or disruption of menstrual periods (called amenorrhea), and loss of bone mass (called osteoporosis). Any one of these conditions can signal that the body's essential nutrients and tissues are being beset by a combination of starvation and overexercising. A female athlete can have any part of the triad, but when all three conditions appear at the same time, it is a health emergency. If you think you have female athlete triad, talk to your school counselor, coach, trainer, a family member, nurse, dietitian, or family doctor.

Anorexia, bulimia, and other eating disorders can be treated with the help of therapists, doctors, and nutritionists. Gymnasts and those around them should be aware of the above warning signs of eating disorders. Gymnasts should diet only with the advice of a professional. Young women in gymnastics often feel the constant stress of having to compete to win. Teen gymnasts are developing a sense of themselves during a period when body image is frequently a concern. The focus for gymnasts with eating disorders becomes food, either the purge of bulimia or the starvation of anorexia. According to a report published in 2014 by the Journal of Sports Sciences, athletes who had eating disorders were more likely to suffer later from depression. With the proper treatment team, a gymnast who has an eating disorder can recover and return to competition.

CHAPTER FOUR

GYMNASTICS EVENTS AND GYMNASTS

There are many annual gymnastics events and competitions that have become notable for giving young gymnasts a forum for performing on the national stage. The Junior Olympic program gives gymnasts the ability to work their way up in skill level, competing in more than one skill level per year, if they wish. Women's artistic events include the Secret US Classic, P&G Gymnastics Championships (sponsored by the company Procter & Gamble), the World Championships, Nastia Liukin Cup (before 2012, called the Nastia Liukin Supergirl Cup), AT&T American Cup, Pacific Rim Gymnastics Championships, Junior Olympic Level 9 Eastern Championships, Junior National Invitation Tournament, Junior Olympic National Championships, National Qualifier/American Classic, and the Women's Olympic Trials. There are many state and regional events that offer gymnasts interscholastic athletic contests. Most state high schools use USA Gymnastics Junior Olympic rules

U.S. gymnast Alex McMurtry performs her floor routine at the 2013 Nastia Liukin Cup. She won the individual all-around title at the competition.

with certain modifications for their girls' gymnastics competitions. For more information about rules and regulations in your state, you can check out the state's high school athletic association's website.

The Amateur Athletic Union (AAU) Gymnastics National Committee encourages participation in gymnastics and has adopted rules and regulations for its competitions at the regional and national levels. These include district championships, state meets, district qualifiers, and regional and national competitions. For district rules, the AAU recommends that you contact your local district. There are three different levels for AAU national level competitions: the AAU Junior Olympic Games, AAU Age Group National Championships, and AAU Winter Nationals. Additional information about the AAU local, district, invitational, regional championship,

Jordyn Wieber of the United States trains for the Olympic Games. Gymnastics has been included in every Olympic competition since 1896 (when men's gymnastics began as an event).

and national championship competitions can be obtained in the National AAU Gymnastics Handbook, published annually (with periodic updates).

ALY RAISMAN

Born in 1994, Alexandra "Aly" Raisman hopes to become the oldest gymnast to make the U.S. women's gymnastics team in the 2016 Olympic Games when they are held in Rio de Janeiro, Brazil. By then she will be twenty-two, and, according to reporter Morty Ain of ESPN, she works on her routine for six days each week so that she can reach her goal of winning a spot on the Olympic team. She also understands that there is a lot of disappointment in the sport and that working so hard all the time has an impact on an individual both mentally and physically. When she is competing, she is totally concentrating on her moves. She told Ain, "When I was competing in the London Olympics during the beam final, there were thousands of screaming people in the stands, but the only voice I could hear was [teammate] McKayla Maroney . . . talking me through the beam routine the whole time." She also noted that she has never had an eating disorder and that instead of being self-conscious about her muscles she has come to love them. She informed Ain, "I don't even think of it as a flaw anymore because it's made me into the athlete that I am."

Gabrielle Douglas competes on the uneven bars at the 2012 Olympics. She is the first African American gymnast in Olympic history to win the gold medal as the all-around champion.

Today's women's artistic gymnastics national teams include girls and women from the states of Arizona, California, Florida, Georgia, Iowa, Kansas, Massachusetts, Minnesota, Missouri, New Jersey, North Carolina, Ohio, and Washington. Some U.S. gymnasts who are fan favorites include Alyssa Baumann, Simone Biles, Jordan Chiles, Nia Dennis, Madison Desch, Gabby Douglas, Brenna Dowell, Norah Flatley, Jazmyn Foberg, Rachel Gowey, McKayla Maroney, Maggie Nichols, Aly Raisman, Kyla Ross, Megan Skaggs, and MyKayla Skinner.

The 2016 Olympic Team Trials in June 2016 in St. Louis, Missouri, for men and in July 2016 in San Jose, California, for women spark high expectations for the U.S. teams. According to *USA Today*, the officials at USA Gymnastics said they "expect

U.S. gymnast Norah Flatley competes in the P&G Gymnastics Championships, also called the USA Gymnastics National Championships.

the women's trials to have a Final Four-like atmosphere in 2016." (The Final Four are the four college basketball teams that qualify for the annual National Collegiate Athletic Association championship tournament.) Gymnasts Gabby Douglas, McKayla Maroney, Aly Raisman, and Kyla Ross are all favored to make the U.S. team. Whatever happens at these events, you can be sure that the arena will be filled with up-and-coming gymnasts and many Olympic medal hopefuls! With the 2016 Summer Olympic Games being held in Rio de Janeiro, Brazil, the excitement for Olympic medals for the U.S. gymnastics team will be at an all-time high.

TIMELINE

1830s Artistic gymnastics is introduced to the United States by immigrants Charles Beck, Charles Follen, and Francis Lieber.

1881 The Bureau of the European Gymnastics Federation (now called the International Gymnastics Federation) is formed, opening the way for international competition.

1896 Men's gymnastics becomes part of the Olympics. Germany dominates the sport.

1928 The first women's gymnastics events are held at the Olympic Games. The Netherlands wins.

1931 Roberta C. Ranck wins the first U.S. All-Around Gymnastics Championship.

1936 U.S. women first compete in gymnastics in the Olympic Games in Berlin, Germany.

1960 Ukrainian Larisa Latynina wins three golds, two silvers, and a bronze medal for gymnastics at the Rome Olympics.

1964 Larisa Latynina completes her Olympic career in gymnastics with more medals than any athlete in Olympic history: nine gold, five silver, and four bronze.

1970 Cathy Rigby wins a silver medal in the balance beam at the World Championships, becoming the first American, man or woman, to win a medal in international competition. The United States Gymnastics Federation, now known as USA Gymnastics, becomes the national governing body of the sport.

1972 Congress passes Title IX of the Education Amendments of 1972. When President Richard Nixon signs the act on July 23, about 31,000 women are involved in college sports; spending on athletic scholarships for women is less than $100,000; and the average number of women's teams at a college is 2.1. Soviet gymnast Olga Korbut wins three gold medals at the Summer Olympics in Munich, Germany.

1976 Romanian Nadia Comaneci becomes the first gymnast to receive a perfect score from the judges, earning a 10.0 on the uneven bars at the Summer Games in Montreal, Canada. She leads Romania to the silver medal in the team competition and takes the individual gold medals on the uneven bars and the balance beam, while also winning the overall individual competition.

1984 Mary Lou Retton wins the gold medal in the all-around in women's gymnastics at the Olympics. She also wins an individual silver medal in the vault and bronze medals in the uneven bars and floor exercise. Her five medals are the most won by any athlete at the 1984 Olympics. She is named the Associated Press Female Athlete of the Year.

1987 The first annual National Girls and Women in Sports Day is celebrated in the United States.

1991 Kim Zmeskal becomes the first American woman to win an all-around World Championship in gymnastics. The U.S. team wins a silver medal in the World Championships, finishing behind the Soviet Union but ahead of the Romanians for the first time.

1992 At fourteen, Kerri Strug becomes the youngest American representing the country at the 1992 Olympic Games in Barcelona. U.S. gymnast Shannon Miller wins five medals at the Barcelona games.

1996 Kerri Strug performs the last vault on an injured ankle during the 1996 Olympic Games and helps the U.S. team, called the Magnificent Seven, clinch the first ever Olympic gold medal in the team competition. Shannon Miller wins the gold medal on the balance beam at the 1996 Olympics.

2004 Carly Patterson wins the gold medal for the all-around title and a silver medal for the balance beam at the 2004 Olympics in Atlanta.

2005 At the World Championships in Melbourne, Australia, the U.S. women's team wins nine out of ten medals.

2006 Shannon Miller is inducted as a member of the Class of 2006 in the International Gymnastics Hall of Fame. The International Gymnastics Federation adopts a new gymnastics scoring system, in which a gymnast's total score is a combination of a score for the difficulty of the routine and one for how well the routine has been executed.

2007 In Stuttgart, Germany, the U.S. women's team wins the gold medal at the World Championships. Shawn Johnson wins the gold medal in the all-around and one in the floor exercise. Nastia Liukin wins the balance beam gold medal and a silver medal on the uneven bars.

2008 The Magnificent Seven, the 1996 US Olympic Team, are inducted into the U.S. Olympic Hall of Fame in June. In August, Nastia Liukin wins the gold medal in the all-around, and Shawn Johnson wins the silver in the all-around at the Olympic Games in Beijing. Liukin wins the silver medals in the uneven bars and balance beam and a bronze in the floor exercise. Johnson wins a gold medal on the balance beam and a silver medal for the floor.

2010 The first Nastia Liukin Cup, hosted by Nastia Liukin, is held. Alicia Sacramone wins the gold medal in the vault at the World Championships in Rotterdam, Netherlands. The U.S. women's team wins the team silver medal.

2011 McKayla Maroney wins the gold medal in the vault at the 2011 World Championships.

2012 The International Gymnastics Federation's World Acrobatic Gymnastics Championships and the World Acrobatic Gymnastics Age Group Competition, hosted by USA Gymnastics, is held in Orlando, Florida, which is the first time the competitions have not been held in Europe. In the Summer Olympic Games in London, the U.S. women's team, called the Fierce Five, wins the team gold medal. Gabby Douglas becomes the first African American gymnast to win the gold medal in the all-around.

2013 Gabby Douglas wins the 2013 Teen Choice Award for best female athlete. Kyla Ross wins gold medals for uneven bars and balance beam and silver medal for all-around at the P&G Championships.

2014 U.S. women's gymnastics team wins the team gold medal at the World Championships.

2015 Simone Biles wins the AT&T American Cup all-around crown in her home state of Texas. The International Gymnastics Federation announces that starting with the Tokyo 2020 Olympics, Olympic gymnastics team event sizes will be cut from five gymnasts to four.

2016 U.S. Olympic Gymnastic Trials are to be held in San Jose, California, in July. The 2016 Summer Olympic Games are to be held in Rio de Janeiro, Brazil, in August.

GLOSSARY

ALL-AROUND GYMNAST The athlete who has the highest total score on each piece of equipment.

ANOREXIA NERVOSA An eating disorder in which a person has an intense fear of getting fat, refuses to eat, and keeps losing weight.

APPARATUS A piece of equipment used in gymnastics competitions, such as the balance beam and vault.

ARRHYTHMIA A physical condition in which the heart beats with an irregular rhythm.

ARTISTIC GYMNASTICS The branch of gymnastics that uses four pieces of equipment and is practiced by women.

BULIMIA NERVOSA An eating disorder in which huge amounts of food are eaten then purged by vomiting, using laxatives, or exercising excessively.

CARTWHEEL The move in which a gymnast turns sideways from a standing position, to a handstand, and then back to a standing position.

CODE OF POINTS The book of rules and regulations for gymnastics.

COMPULSORIES Set routines that contain specific movements required of all gymnasts.

DISMOUNT To leave an apparatus at the end of a routine; usually done with flare.

ELITE GYMNAST A gymnast who is recognized as an international competitor.

EVENTS Routines performed by gymnasts on different apparatuses. Women have four events: the balance beam, vault, uneven bars, and floor.

EXECUTION The performance of a routine. Form, style, and the technique used to complete the skills constitute the level of execution of an exercise.

FEMALE ATHLETE TRIAD The combination of three conditions—an eating disorder, amenorrhea (when a girl or woman who is not pregnant stops having menstrual periods), and osteoporosis—any one or all of which can affect a female athlete.

HANDGRIPS The leather straps that a gymnast wears on her hands to help her have a firm hold on the bar.

HANDSPRING Springing off the hands by putting the weight on the arms and using a strong push from the shoulders; can be done either forward or backward.

HANDSTAND A movement where the gymnast balances on the hands, with the body straight above the hands.

OPTIONALS Personally designed routines that show off the gymnast to her best advantage.

RIP A piece of skin that tears off the hand or wrist from blisters.

ROUTINE A combination of stunts displaying a full range of skills on one apparatus.

SOMERSAULT Any movement in which the gymnast rotates in a full circle along the ground or in the air.

SPOTTER Someone who stands ready to assist a gymnast if she needs help.

STRESS FRACTURE A very small crack in a bone, usually caused by repetitive physical force, such as jumping up and down, in the legs or feet.

TUCK A position in which the knees and hips are bent and drawn into the chest; the body is bent at the waist.

FOR MORE INFORMATION

Amateur Athletic Union of the United States, Inc. (AAU)
P.O. Box 22409
Lake Buena Vista, FL 32830
(407) 934-7200
Website: http://aausports.org
The AAU was established in 1888 to create standards in amateur
    sports. Today it focuses on providing sports programs for
    people of all ages. Its Gymnastics National Committee encour-
    ages participation in gymnastics programs at all levels.

Gymnastics Canada
1900 City Park Drive, Suite 120
Ottawa, ON K1J 1A3
Canada
(613) 748-5637
Website: http://www.gymcan.org
This organization governs the sport of gymnastics in Canada and
    works closely with provincial federations and clubs to help all
    participants in the sport.

Gymnastics Ontario
3 Concorde Gate, Suite 214
Toronto, ON M3C 3N7
Canada
(416) 426-7100
Website: http://www.gymnasticsontario.ca
This organization governs the sport of gymnastics in Ontario and
supports member clubs in providing programs and services.

International Gymnastics Federation (FIG)
Avenue de la Gare 12
CP 630
1001 Lausanne
Switzerland
Website: http://www.fig-gymnastics.com
The Fédération Internationale de Gymnastique (FIG) was established in 1881. It is the world governing body for gymnastics and the Olympic competitions and World Gymnastic Championships.

National Collegiate Athletic Association (NCAA)
700 West Washington Street
P.O. Box 6222
Indianapolis, IN 46206-6222
(317) 917-6222
Website: http://www.ncaa.org
The NCAA provides college gymnastics programs in Divisions I, II, and III and holds regional and other championship events.

USA Gymnastics
132 East Washington Street, Suite 700
Indianapolis, IN 46204
(317) 237-5050
Website: http://www.usagym.org
This organization governs the sport of gymnastics in the United States. It selects and trains national teams and sets the rules and regulations for the sport in the United States. The Junior Olympic program is divided into the developmental, compulsory, and optional segments. The organization also provides information for member clubs, fans, and gymnasts across the country.

U.S. Olympic Committee (USOC)
One Olympic Plaza
Colorado Springs, CO 80909
(888) 222-2313
Website: http://www.teamusa.org
The USOC serves as the Olympic committee and the Paralympic
    committee for the United States. It is responsible for training
    and funding U.S. teams for the Olympic, Paralympic, Youth
    Olympic, Pan American, and Parapan American Games. It
    supports the Olympic Movement and oversees the U.S. process
    for making bids to host the games.

Women's Sports Foundation
(800) 227-3988
Website: http://action.womenssportsfoundation.org
This organization was founded in 1974 by Billie Jean King, the
    tennis legend. It promotes sports and physical activities for
    girls and women and supports the educational program
    GoGirlGo! and the grant program Sports 4 Life.

WEBSITES

Because of the changing nature of Internet links, Rosen
Publishing has developed an online list of websites related to
the subject of this book. This site is updated regularly. Please
use this link to access the list:

http://www.rosenlinks.com/IX/Gym

FOR FURTHER READING

Beim, Gloria, and Ruth Winter. *The Female Athlete's Body Book: How to Prevent and Treat Sports Injuries in Women and Girls*. Chicago, IL: Contemporary Books, 2003.

Brown, Heather. *How to Improve at Gymnastics*. St. Catharines, ON and New York, NY: Crabtree Publishing Company, 2009.

Douglas, Gabrielle, and Michelle Burford. *Grace, Gold, and Glory: My Leap of Faith*. Grand Rapids, MI: Zondervan, 2012.

Gifford, Clive. *Gymnastics*. Mankato, MN: Amicus, 2012.

Johnson, Shawn. *Shawn Johnson, Olympic Champion: Stories Behind the Smile*. Des Moines, IA: Lexicon, 2008.

Jones, Jen. *Gymnastics Events: Floor, Vault, Bars, and Beam*. Mankato, MN: Capstone Press, 2007.

Kleinbaum, N. H. *The Magnificent Seven: The Authorized Story of American Gold*. New York, NY: Bantam Books, 1998.

Kosara, Tori. *Gabby Douglas: Going for Gold*. New York, NY: Scholastic, 2013.

Lawrence, Blythe. *Girls' Gymnastics*. North Mankato, MN: ABDO Publishing, 2014.

Le Boutillier, Nate. *Gymnastics* (Summer Olympic Legends). Mankato, MN: Creative Education, 2012.

Miller, Shannon, and Danny Peary. *It's Not Perfect: Competing for My Country and Fighting for My Life*. New York, NY: Thomas Dunne Books, 2015.

Nixon, James, and Bobby Humphrey. *Gymnastics*. London, UK: Franklin Watts, 2014.

Olsen, Leigh. *Going for Gold: The 2008 U.S. Women's Gymnastics Team*. New York, NY: Price Stern Sloan, 2008.

Peters, Stephanie True, and Matt Christopher. *Great Moments in the Summer Olympics*. New York, NY: Little Brown and Company, 2012.

Readhead, Lloyd. *Gymnastics: Skills, Techniques, Training*. E-book. New York, NY: Crowood, 2013.

Savage, Jeff. *Top 25 Gymnastics Skills, Tips, and Tricks*. Berkeley Heights, NJ: Enslow Publishers, 2012.

Sey, Jennifer. *Chalked Up: Inside Elite Gymnastics' Merciless Coaching, Overzealous Parents, Eating Disorders, and Elusive Olympic Dreams*. New York, NY: William Morrow, 2008.

Tieck, Sarah. *Gabby Douglas*. Minneapolis, MN: ABDO Publishing, 2013.

INDEX

ABOUT THE AUTHORS

Glen F. Stanley is a devoted gymnastics fan and has a daughter who competes in the sport at the local high school. He has previously written about baseball and resides in upstate New York.

Ann Wesley lives and works in Bloomington, Indiana, and is an avid sports fan. She has a degree in journalism from Indiana University and has written for newspapers and magazines. Wesley currently works as a director of a Web design company.

PHOTO CREDITS